Body Parts

Becoming the Unified Body of Christ

Lionel Childress

Sermon To Book
www.sermontobook.com

Body Parts / Lionel Childress
ISBN-13: 978-1-945793-32-5
ISBN-10: 1-945793-32-5

Giving all honor and glory to God, I dedicate this book:

To the love of my life of forty years, to my seven natural children and adopted children, and to all my grandchildren and my adopted grandchildren.

To those who have gone to glory, to the best sons and daughters-in-laws, and to all of my sons and daughters in the Lord.

To my pastors, churches, apostles, Drs. and bishops, chiefs, arch bishops, priests, prophets, teachers, deacons, mothers, singers, musicians, all positions of help, and members.

To the hero of my life, my dad, to the best mom in the world, and to my mother in law.

To my sisters and brothers, and to their husbands and wives and their kids. To my wife's sisters and brothers, and their kids. To all our cousins, uncles, aunties, and friends.

To Childress Deliverance Temple, Childress Covenant International Churches, my NB88 family, and all our churches in the United States, Africa, the Bahamas, and elsewhere.

To all who stood with us, to all who stand with us, to all who started with us. To all who touched us in God's grace. To all colors and denominations who loved on us, before and now.

And to the only other man I call "Pops"—I dedicate this book to you, sir. Glory.

Special thanks to my wife, Lady Jeanette M. Childress; my brother, Dr. Robert E. Childress; my senior son-in-God, Apostle Raymond Wells; my second-eldest son, Bishop Darrell Blair; my third eldest, Apostle Brian A. Wilson; Pastor Lionel Childress, Jr.; my son-in-law Bishop Cedrick Major; my grandson Pastor Joshua B. Campbell; my daughter, administrator Sharonda L. Campbell; my daughter, recording artist Shatrisha Green; my daughter, psalmist Shanta McLane; my grandson, drummer Jordan Campbell; my grandson, Jireh Campbell; and my daughter, my Taylor, Shakiniah Major.

And thanks also to Regional Leader Apostle James Dancy, Regional Leader Apostle Jerome Steele, Regional Leader Overseer Reginald Robinson, Regional Leader Bishop Merdice Bartly, Regional Leader Apostle Kevin More, Business Bishop Emmanuel Omercre, my NB88 family, Childress Deliverance Temple, International Prophet Apostle Lee Tyson, and psalmist Sean Hall.

In memory of my daughter Shantoqua, my son Schon, my mom Marlene, my dad Tommie, my mother Odesa, my brother Donell, and my God-son Lionel Rhodes.

CONTENTS

A Note from the Author

Thank you for purchasing *Body Parts: Becoming the Unified Body of Christ*.

Accompanying each main chapter of the book is a set of reflective questions to help you deepen and apply your understanding of what it means for Christians to be the undivided Body of Christ.

Each workbook section includes questions for discussion or reflection as well as a practical action step. These sections are a practical tool to help you get the most out of the book, and I recommend you go through these sections with a pen in order to write your thoughts in the areas provided.

Whether you read the book and work through the questions by yourself, with a friend, or with a study group, I hope you will enjoy the experience and grow more fully into your place in the Body of Christ.

WELCOME

Introduction

From the early days of the Christian church to modern day, church leaders have wrestled with the same recurring problem: Division. Contrary to what some may think, church division is not because of a disagreement about religion; that is too simple.

Division occurs when God's people put their preconceived ideas above a love for truth. Personal agendas and self-will take precedence above God's commands. People readily follow doctrines invented by men but found nowhere in the Bible. They may determine their beliefs by other people—family or friends, the latest trendy book, even false teachers or preachers—but this is not where truth is found.

*Your word is truth. — **John 17:17 (NKJV)***

*Every word of God is flawless; he is a shield to those who take refuge in him. — **Proverbs 30:5 (NIV)***

Thy word is true from the beginning: and every one of thy righteous judgments endureth for ever. ***— Psalm 119:160 (KJV)***

The word of God is the only plumb line for truth in a mixed-up, humanistic world, and should be what unifies the body of Christ. Put simply, division in the church is caused when God's people are not willing to diligently obey His word.

Because of division, the church has splintered into piles of denominations, each formed to smooth out the areas of disagreement. The result? The body of Christ is broken, not unified and ineffective. The world looks in on the church, and should find a place of hope, of restoration, and of love but finds disagreement, fighting, and sometimes hatred.

What Jesus left on this earth to draw nations to Him is a light that seems to be flickering out. Though often not discussed, many within the church are sensing the same thing: the universal church is sick.

The prophets looked forward to a time where there would be one church, not many churches.

In the last days the mountain of the LORD's temple will be established as the highest of the mountains; it will be exalted above the hills, and all nations will stream to it.
— Isaiah 2:2 (NIV)

Isaiah foretold one temple, or church, that would be exalted over all others, not a myriad of denominations. The promised church that Jesus said He would build in Matthew 16:18 was always singular. This one church belongs to Christ, the "firstborn" from the dead.

> *And he is the head of the body, the church; he is the beginning and the firstborn from among the dead, so that in everything he might have the supremacy.* — ***Colossians 1:18 (NIV); see also Hebrews 12:23***

The existence of a multitude of churches—all believing different things and all fighting amongst themselves—is not what existed in those few years after Jesus died and resurrected.

How did this happen? When did God's church become so disunified? How is it that the "tradition of men" (Colossians 2:8) has come to reign supreme among churches of Christ today, above even Christ Himself?

Early on, the apostle Paul was concerned. He warned of this problem, speaking of a "falling away" that would occur (2 Thessalonians 2:1-12) and that false prophets would arise who would preach a different gospel that would turn believers away from "Him who called you in the grace of Christ." (Galatians 2:6 NKJV). He knew some would use deceit and the tradition of men to divide the church (Acts 20:30-31). Gnosticism was prevalent in Paul's time. This group believed they had been given a "higher knowledge." Jesus was a spirit being, they thought, who was sent by God to bestow knowledge to humans, that they might escape the agonies of life on earth. This movement stirred up dissension in the early church, wooing Christians towards false doctrine.

In 70 AD, Rome destroyed Jerusalem, thus, the Christian movement—which consisted of both Jewish and Gentile believers—was scattered and divided. As early as 110 AD, there is evidence of a departure of the original foundation and organization of the body of Christ. Pauline Christians and Gnostic Christianity were left as the dominant groups. The Roman Empire recognized Pauline Christianity as a valid religion in 313 AD, and soon any involvement with Jewish practices—even though this was what the church was founded on—was deemed "*Judaizing.*"

A split between Roman Catholic and Eastern Orthodox churches in the early 1000s AD marked the very first major division in Christianity and the beginning of denominations. The Protestant Reformation followed in the 16th century, marking the beginning of denominationalism, as we know today.

What Paul tried so desperately to prevent is what we know today as the church—believers all around the world who love Jesus, but are huddled in their own like-minded communities operating apart from the whole.

But all is not lost. It is possible to exist as a unified body of believers. To restore church unity, we must address the root problems causing our division and zealously guard against letting our denominational opinions take precedence over the Lord's truth and the work of His Spirit.

There is a solution, but it is radical. It involves a complete shift in our thinking and an honest evaluation of our hearts. It involves a return to the purity of the Word of

God and a belief that God can indeed unify us. Only then will the church be a force to be reckoned with.

> *Thus says the LORD: Stand in the ways and see, and ask for the old paths, where the good way is, and walk in it; Then you will find rest for your souls. But they said, 'We will not walk in it.'* ***— Jeremiah 6:16 (NKJV)***

WORKBOOK

Introduction Questions

Question: Where in your church or community do you see division in the body of Christ?

____
____
____
____
____
____
____
____
____
____
____
____

Question: What are the sources of these divisions?

____
____
____
____
____
____

____

____

____

____

____

____

Action: Division in the church is caused when God's people are not willing to diligently obey His word. Communities of those who love Jesus ought to cease huddling in isolation and instead exist as a unified body of believers. To restore church unity, we must address the root problems causing our division and zealously guard against letting our denominational opinions overshadow the Lord's truth and the work of His Spirit. Return individually and collectively to the purity of the Word of God and a belief that God can indeed unify us. Only then will the church be a force to be reckoned with!

Introduction Notes

CHAPTER ONE

Body Parts

Endeavoring to keep the unity of the Spirit in the bond of peace. There is one body and one Spirit, just as you were called in one hope of your calling; one Lord, one faith, one baptism; one God and Father of all, who is above all, and through all, and in you all. — ***Ephesians 4:3-6 (NKJV)***

Mother Marshall walked everywhere she went. One hot summer day, she stopped while passing by my family's house. My dad and I were working on the roof, placing shingles in the overwhelming heat. Mother Marshall called to my dad, saying, "I had to stop!" She then pointed at me. "The sun sits over his head in a way that marks him! God told me to come and tell you that he is destined for the gospel ministry!"

The sun shined on me that day in a way that made me feel strange. And though I didn't think much of it at the time, the experience changed my life. At just twelve-years-old, I received a call from God and I've been preaching ever since.

A Body in Strife

Years later, I had another divine encounter—a vision—but this time there was no light over my head "marking me." In this vision, I knew deep in my soul that God wasn't pleased with His people. Suddenly it was revealed that this "crowd" I was seeing was the universal church. God was despondent because He couldn't do great things with His church when they were quarrelling amongst themselves.

The biblical imagery of the body signifies the spiritual body of Jesus Christ, which is inevitably a diverse group. Writing to the Corinthian church, Paul affirmed this by saying:

> *Now you are the body of Christ, and each one of you is a part of it. —* ***1 Corinthians 12:27 (NIV)***

In biblical times and in Greco-Roman literature, the term "body" referred to a community. The usage is even found in the writings of Aristotle in reference to the state, a social unit, or even the cosmos. For the apostle Paul to use the phrase "the body of Christ" represents the concept of a whole.

Like a human body that needs to be cared for, the body of Christ is a body that must be cared for by its members. The body gathers for worship, but continues to function in the world through the diverse vocations, nationalities, and personalities of its members.

Not all people who make up the church body look like

each other. Yet, however different we might be, we were not made to destroy or attack each other. We were made to proclaim the gospel as one unique, unified body. When we focus more on our differences rather than on our unified mission, we end up looking more like that unhappy group in my vision than the joyful people of the gospel ministry.

Paul often used the phrase "body of Christ" in connection with Eucharistic celebrations. For example, he wrote, "The bread that we break a participation in the body of Christ?" (1 Corinthians 10:16 NIV). This phrase was immediately followed by the verse, "Because there is one loaf, we, who are many, are one body…" (1 Corinthians 10:17 NIV). It seems like Paul was using the concept of a unified social unit to illustrate what exactly the body of Christ was to *look* like.

Should the phrase "the body of Christ" be taken metaphorically or literally? Certainly, the body of Christ does not only refer to the literal risen body of Jesus. The term "body" can't be restricted to the material substance of a person. Consider the following:

The main portion of an object can be described as its "body." For example, the body of a letter or the body of the car. There are heavenly bodies, bodies of law, and bodies of water. Therefore, to speak of the church as "the body of Christ" as a community found within the whole of Christ, should not be found unusual or considered *only* metaphorical.

Eduard Schweizer writes that for Paul the image "is more than a metaphor," for "Christ *himself* is the body into which all members are baptized" (emphasis added).[1] But the term lends itself well for metaphorical purposes, too, allowing for analogies to parts of the body:

> *For the body is not one member, but many. If the foot shall say, Because I am not the hand, I am not of the body; is it therefore not of the body? And if the ear shall say, Because I am not the eye, I am not a part of the body; is it therefore not of the body? If the whole body were an eye, where were the hearing? If the whole were hearing, where were the smelling? But now hath God set the members every one of them in the body, as it hath pleased him. And if they were all one member, where were the body? But now are they many members, yet but one body. And the eye cannot say unto the hand, I have no need of thee: nor again the head to the feet, I have no need of you. Nay, much more those members of the body, which seem to be more feeble, are necessary: and those members of the body, which we think to be less honourable, upon these we bestow more abundant honour; and our uncomely parts have more abundant comeliness. For our comely parts have no need: but God hath tempered the body together, having given more abundant honour to that part which lacked. That there should be no schism in the body; but that the members should have the same care for one another. And whether one member suffer, all the members suffer with it; or one member be honoured, all the members rejoice with it. Now ye are the body of Christ, and members in particular.* — ***1 Corinthians 12:14-27 (KJV)***

But this figurative imagery should be considered secondary. According to Paul, the body of Christ is first of all the eschatological (end times) community of the Spirit, which exists already in the present world.

Those within the "body" share His literal, physical future. The kingdom of God is also you and me.

The kingdom of God is in your midst. — ***Luke 17:21 (NIV)***

What God has done in and through Christ's redemptive death and resurrection is ours. As we have "died to the law through the body of Christ," so we belong... "to him who was raised from the dead" (Romans 7:4 NIV).

For the Completeness of the Body

It might trouble some that collectively churches seem to have a myriad of different agendas. How can these vast differences be indicative of the one body of Christ? Doesn't this reflect a disjoined body of Christ?

On the contrary. We should consider it *good* that every church has a different calling and assignment, because though different, they all are intended to work for the same unity and the same completeness of the body of Christ as a whole. God calls us to celebrate our unique gifting, while also remaining united in Christ.

The Bible clearly speaks of one gospel and of one Lord. However, it doesn't take long to come across people (or entire denominations) saying that Jesus is different for every person. Denominations squabble over whom exactly that Lord is! We fight over the name of Jesus—whether He is Jehovah, Jehovah Jireh, or Elohim. Then, we'll fight over the day to have church, the way to dress, and how to pray. Thus, the church, which is supposed to be unified, ends up divided.

Individual believers have different gifts. Isaiah communicates God as the master potter, creating individual and unique pieces of art—no two pots are the same (Isaiah 64:8). Paul teaches that in the body there are apostles, prophets, teachers, and miracles workers:

> *Now you are Christ's body, and individually members of it. And God has appointed in the church, first apostles, second prophets, third teachers, then miracles, then gifts of healings, helps, administrations, various kinds of tongues. All are not apostles, are they? All are not prophets, are they? All are not teachers, are they? All are not workers of miracles, are they? All do not have gifts of healings, do they? All do not speak with tongues, do they? All do not interpret, do they? But earnestly desire the greater gifts.* — ***1 Corinthians 12:27-31 (NASB)***

Peter wrote that God has given each of us a gift from His great variety of spiritual gifts:

> *As each one has received a special gift, employ it in serving one another as good stewards of the manifold grace of God. Whoever speaks, is to do so as one who is speaking the utterances of God; whoever serves is to do so as one who is serving by the strength which God supplies; so that in all things God may be glorified through Jesus Christ, to whom belongs the glory and dominion forever and ever. Amen.*
> ***—1 Peter 4:10-11 (NASB)***

In the midst of these exhausting arguments of "distinct yet unified," God is trying to tell us something: there is only *one* Lord, *one* faith and *one* baptism. This is what should knit the body of Christ together. A unified body is the only thing that will reflect the God of the universe to a broken and dying world.

Chapter Summary

Though there are many followers of Christ and many denominations that hold differing opinions, God did not intend for believers and churches to operate independently from one another. The church Jesus established was to exist as a whole in heart, mind, and spirit. How can this possibly be manifested when there is so much strife in the body? In the following chapter, we will look into God's plan for unity and what this means for the follower of Jesus.

WORKBOOK

Chapter One Questions

Question: Should the phrase "the body of Christ" be taken metaphorically or literally? Explain your response.

Question: What does your church see as its calling or assignment within the body of Christ?

____

Question: How does your church work with other churches in the body of Christ? What more could your church do in this regard?

____

Action: Paul used the phrase "the body of Christ" to represents the concept of Jesus' followers as a united whole. However different we might be, we were not made to destroy or attack each other. Instead, consider it *good* that every church has a different calling and assignment, because though different, they all are intended to work together for Christ's purposes. Avoid strife with other believers, other churches, and other denominations, for there is only *one* Lord, *one* faith, and *one* baptism. Work toward unity!

Chapter One Notes

CHAPTER TWO

United by the Spirit

If each of us is different, how can the body of Christ stay united? Paul, writing from prison (Ephesians 6:21-22), writes to the Ephesians praising God for who He is and what He has done, as evidenced in the person and work of Jesus Christ and in the gospel, through the unity of the body of Christ in the Holy Spirit. Paul exhorted his disciples to "Make every effort to keep the unity of the Spirit..." (Ephesians 4:3a; see also Romans 2:11, 1 Timothy 5:21).

Yet, Paul continues by explaining that this body is held together with the "bond of peace," and in a single hope (Ephesians 4:3-4).

> *There is one body and one Spirit, just as you were called to one hope when you were called; one Lord, one faith, one baptism; one God and Father of all, who is over all and through all and in all.* — ***Ephesians 4:4-6 (NIV)***

Seven times in Ephesians 4:4-6, Paul repeats the number "one": one body, one Spirit, one hope, one Lord, one faith, one baptism, one God and Father. For one congregation to say to another that they are unable to fellowship with one another is not in alignment with the Word of God. Paul is describing one wonderful result of the unity that the Word and Spirit produced: a whole united company of Christians functioning as a vibrant and active church. They are a force to be reckoned with in this world, because when operating in the Spirit, they are not at war with one another. Their energies are spent looking up to heaven, waiting for their "redemption [that is] drawing near" (Luke 21:28) and looking outward to others who do not yet possess this gift.

Let's consider God's establishment of the church. To do this, we must define what a "church" actually is—more than a building where Christians gather to worship God. The word "church" comes from the Greek word *ekklesia*, which is defined as "an assembly" or "called-out ones." The root meaning of "church" is not that of a building, but of people.

It is ironic that when you ask people what church they attend, they usually identify a building. In Romans 16:5 Paul writes to "greet the church that *is in their house*." He isn't saying, "Greet the house." The church, then, is a body of believers.

With this definition, let's consider the establishment of God's church. At the very beginning, the "church" was small–Adam and Eve. It grew to eight, with Noah and his family, and then through the line of Abraham blossomed into the great nation of Israel. Though the nation was massive, the real body of believers during Old Testament times was consistently a tiny remnant.

> *And Isaiah cries out concerning Israel: 'Though the number of the sons of Israel be as the sand of the sea, only a remnant of them will be saved...' —* ***Romans 9:27 (ESV)***

After God poured out His Spirit at Pentecost, the gospel of Christ began to spread like wildfire out from Judea to Africa and Europe. Today, the church exists across the entire globe. The central unifying entity in this global body is Christ.

One man told the story of reading a Christian book while on a plane, flying across America. The man beside him noticed, and began to talk to him. It was not long before they discovered they were both Christians. They had connected with someone else in the body having never known the other before that moment.

The church is a body, not a computer. It is not the joining together of various parts. It is one body that has grown by the multiplication of cells.

> *It is not a question of fingers being stuck on hands, and hands to forearms, and so on. It is all one. All the parts come out of an original cell, as it were an original germ of life, and they are all extensions and manifestations of that. The unity in the church is like that, and whether we like it or not, we have to face that fact. —* ***D. Martin Lloyd-Jones***[2]

This is the background in which Paul's words "the body of Christ" are set. Where, then, is there room for focusing on petty differences when God himself is calling us together through one Spirit, in peace and hope? Just as you or I take care of our own bodies by going to the doctor when we are sick, or brushing our teeth or exercising, we must also care for others in the body. We are one.

God isn't asking for mere servants, but sons and daughters (John 1:12-13). He wants His children to exist as a loving family. God desires for His people to be connected to one another through Him, the One Father of all races and nationalities, of all denominations and traditions who confess His Name.

It's so easy to focus on the church's diversity in a negative light, fighting and rejecting others because they're different. Yet God tells us that He alone is the God and Father of us all. God is above all, and through all and in all, calling us to be one with Him (Ephesians 4:6).

Unity Amidst Diversity

Paul used the metaphor of the body in 1 Corinthians 12:14-27 to communicate to the Corinthians the fundamental importance of unity amidst diversity in Christ (1 Corinthians 12). He described a body made up of diverse elements. According to Paul, unity among these diverse elements comes through the deep sharing of a relationship of mutual responsibility that includes the various members of the body of Christ.

This is similar to the picture of biblical marriage. A man and woman come together—unique and diverse in their personalities, gender, gifts, and passions—but when the two individuals commit to marriage, the Bible says, "'and the two will become one flesh'? So they are no longer two, but one flesh" (Matthew 19:5-6 NIV). Do the man and the woman cease to exist as individuals? Of course not! The woman is still a woman, and the man is still a man. She may be extroverted, and he may be reserved. She may love to teach, and he might have a servant heart. But according to God, their distinctness is unified into one Body, joined together for the magnificent purpose of glorifying Him.

However, the diversity God intended to bring blessing to the marriage, if not checked, can actually evolve into discord. If one spouse does not allow the other to be who God created him to be, tries to control the other, or exist in a place of superiority above the other, tension surfaces. Eventually, separation can occur. What God joined as one for His purposes becomes dysfunctional and purposeless.

In order for authentic unity to become a reality, every part of the body must judge its distinctive position and examine its faithfulness to unity in terms of the ministry and mission of Christ.

Paul was well aware of the condition of the Corinthian church. Factions existed, opinions were strong, and interpretation of Scripture varied. In 1 Corinthians 1:10-17, Paul challenged these early Christians to overcome rising dissension and division to preserve and protect the intended picture of unity and interpersonal faithfulness to the watchful world.

Although some would have liked to claim Paul's support for their particular position, Paul refused to become part of their bickering and divisions and reprimanded those who did, and harshly. He appealed to the church in the name of the Lord Jesus Christ to be united:

> *I appeal to you, brothers and sisters, in the name of our Lord Jesus Christ, that all of you agree with one another in what you say and that there be no divisions among you, but that you be perfectly united in mind and thought. My brothers and sisters, some from Chloe's household have informed me that there are quarrels among you. What I mean is this: One of you says, "I follow Paul"; another, "I follow Apollos"; another, "I follow Cephas"; still another, "I follow Christ."*
>
> *Is Christ divided? Was Paul crucified for you? Were you baptized in the name of Paul? I thank God that I did not baptize any of you except Crispus and Gaius, so no one can say that you were baptized in my name. (Yes, I also baptized the household of Stephanas; beyond that, I don't remember if I baptized anyone else.) For Christ did not send me to baptize, but to preach the gospel—not with wisdom and eloquence, lest the cross of Christ be emptied of its power. —* ***Corinthians 1:10-17 (NIV)***

Paul was aware that the divisions among the Corinthians were deeply rooted in disagreements on nationalism, politics, culture or theology. In fact, politics in the church of Paul's day were based on class and economic status. How true is this of churches today?

Disagreements on these matters fester, often to the point where individuals—and often entire denominations—simply cannot fellowship with one another anymore. This was what Paul was so concerned about.

The beautiful, God-designed diversity within the Corinthian church had become litigious and conflicted. This is why Paul appealed with such fervor to the "body of Christ" metaphor (1 Corinthians 12:27), finding it helpful in communicating with the Corinthians the concept of unity and diversity Christ.

A perfect example of unity amidst diversity is the Trinity. Though the Father, the Son and the Holy Spirit exist as unique persons with specific roles, through the bond of love they too are one.

Paul also cites the relationship between Jews and Gentiles within the body as an example of distinction for unified purpose. We will touch on this more in a later chapter.

Jesus Christ Himself, the God-man, overcame human regulations and rules, brought divine healing and peace to downtrodden men and rose to conquer death, hell and the grave. The one in whom our salvation has been secured has crushed the walls of separation and opened the door to a life of oneness with Him and with each other. That's true unity amidst diversity. God has made us sons and daughters through the uniting work of Jesus Christ (Galatians 4:5).

> *But to each one of us grace was given according to the measure of Christ's gift. Therefore He says: "When He ascended on high, He led captivity captive, and gave gifts to men." (Now this, "He ascended"—what does it mean but that He also first descended into the lower parts of the earth? He who descended is also the One who ascended far above all the heavens, that He might fill all things.)* — ***Ephesians 4:7-10 (NKJV)***

Chapter Summary

God established the church to be a body of believers with distinct gifts, personalities, and passions held together with the bond of peace under one Lord, Jesus Christ. There is no room for division in this body. Like a marriage where each spouse brings their unique self to be established as one unified body, so too is the church. God's desire for the body of Christ is to be unified in its diversity, not divided. With so many differences, however, it may seem near impossible for this kind of intimate unity to ever truly be manifested. Is it possible? True unity in the Body can only be manifested with the grace of God, as we'll see in the next chapter.

WORKBOOK

Chapter Two Questions

Question: What is your identity or in Christ? What is your distinct position in the body of Christ?

Question: How, specifically, can you more fully embrace your identity and role in the body of Christ?

Question: How faithful are you and your church to the principle and goal of unity in Christ?

Action: The Word and Spirit produce unity: a whole, united company of Christians functioning as a vibrant and active church. Embrace your identity as a child in God's family and act in love toward your brothers and sisters in Christ. As part of the body of Christ, reflect on your distinctive position in the body and evaluate your faithfulness to unity in terms of the ministry and mission of Christ.

Chapter Two Notes

CHAPTER THREE

A Measure of Grace

But to each one of us grace has been given as Christ apportioned it. — ***Ephesians 4:7 (NIV)***

Is it possible to attain the type of unity among diversity spoken of in the word of God? Yes it is, but only through the grace and power of the Lord Jesus Christ.

Paul reiterates in Ephesians 4:7 that each follower of Jesus has been given grace according to the measure of the gift of Christ, grace given unto salvation.

Each one of us. At first this statement seems to wipe out the image unity Paul has just outlined. Yes, all believers are one in Christ. But even though we are all of one family, we are not identical.

This is the very point that Paul has been stressing in Ephesians—Jews and Gentiles in one body, but still composed of different individuals. The church is made of people who are different in many ways, whether economically or ethnically, but they are still one in Christ. Here, Paul introduces diversity within the background of unity that comprehends distinction for and with a common goal: *Christ.*

Believers are fundamentally one, but also vastly different. We must keep this principle of "unity in diversity" in the forefront of our heart and mind. This magnificent diversity does not destroy the unity. Likewise, the unity does not do away with the diversity.

There is also grace given for unity in the body of Christ. God knew before the creation of the world that this concept would be hard for humankind to receive and embrace. Paul himself had the grace to reach out to the Gentiles, though he was Jewish. Peter, a Gentile, was empowered with God's grace to be the apostle for the Jews. John the Baptist responded in God's grace to be the forerunner of Jesus Christ. Consider also Moses, Elisha, Elijah and David. Each of these men possessed the grace to call those around them into a more powerful and beautiful unity rooted in the body of the Lord Jesus Christ.

God has given to every man a measure of grace (Ephesians 4:7). This is the only way unity and diversity can coexist in the body of Christ. In the original language, this word "grace" (Gr. *charis*) means "to rejoice" or "to be glad." In this context, grace refers to God's unmerited favor and supernatural enablement and empowerment for salvation and for daily sanctification.

When we begin to understand the word "grace", there is a rejoicing in our heart. And so, to an extent grace can be defined by what it causes—joy, pleasure, delight, gratification, favor and acceptance.

"Measure" refers to a measure of capacity, or the idea of portioning something out. Thus, the grace that exists in a unified body is not so much the grace that saves, but the grace that enables a person to live the supernatural life as a believer, and in context, to exercise one's spiritual gifts. As Paul writes in Romans, "We have different gifts, according to the grace given to each of us." (Romans 12:6 NIV, emphasis added).

Jesus Christ is the head of that Body and as such He is the giver of the variety of gifts that are enjoyed by every member of the church. This principle guarantees the unity in the diversity!

Moses was too afraid to speak, and yet God used him mightily to lead the nation of Israel out from bondage under the Egyptians. Abraham was a simple man, who believed God to be true to His word, and from Him came a great nation. David was a songwriter and King, Rahab was a prostitute and Jesus' disciples were fisherman, tax collectors and doctors. God used each person with their diverse gifts and personalities to cause His purposes to come to pass. Much like these great heroes of the faith, God knows how to empower each of His children to do His work in their own unique way.

Removing the Sting of Death

Wayne Barber tells a story that took place during World War I. There was a tradition in the towns, particularly in France. During the war, cities often had to themselves. Therefore, their little army was the army of that particular city. They had a tradition. These walled cities had walkways stretching over huge gates. When the group of army men returned from battle, the people would climb on top of that gate. A choir would chant. Men returned wounded, broken and bleeding from battle, but they all came back waving their country's flag—they had won the victory! The people on top of the wall would shout, "What right do you have to enter through these gates?" These war-torn men would hold up the hands of the wounded and bleeding. They would raise that flag and say, "We have been to battle, and we have won the victory!" The gates would swing open, and the victors would walk through streets lined with people showering them with hallelujahs! Victory had been won.

This story paints a picture of the rejoicing that occurred when Jesus returned after He ascended to heaven. The heavenly host of angels rejoiced. What right does Jesus have to enter the gates? With His sacrifice on Calvary, He has every right. The gates of heaven swung open that day when the Lord Jesus marched triumphantly before the Father and sat at His right Hand. If Jesus had not ascended, His people would not have received by grace the many gifts He promised. And there would be *no Body.* It cost God everything for us to have the gift of diversity.

Jesus said in John 14, "I must go to My Father." But why? So the Holy Spirit might come. He is the gift. Grasp the wonderful picture here of what Christ has done for us.

> *Without the ascension, there would never be a Christ who could send His Holy Spirit, the ultimate Gift, who in turn could display all the different gifts. The Holy Spirit is the one who is going to be making sure He carries out God's desires Now, as Lord of the Universe, He qualifies to give gifts unto men. —**Wayne Barber**[3]*

The original Greek language is powerful, and brings great insight into what happened at Jesus' victorious entrance into heaven. In this verse, Paul uses the Greek word *doma. Doma* is a word that means "present" or "gift".

The moment Jesus entered heaven to be presented before the throne of God as an acceptable offering, the ancient prophecy of David was fulfilled.

> *When you ascended on high, you took many captives; you received gifts from people, even from the rebellious—that you, LORD God, might dwell there.* — **Psalm 68:18 (NIV)**

This messianic psalm of victory praises God for deliverance. Jesus led "captivity captive." The inferences drawn from the triumphal return of the King are: (1) the thought of victory; and (2) the assignment of gifts.

To take "many captives," signifies that Christ conquered the allied principalities and powers. He defeated the devil, and put an end to sin and death.

What a cost it was for us to have our gifts! Jesus had to go to the cross! Jesus had to resurrect! Jesus had to ascend! Jesus had to go into the presence of the Father before the Spirit could come, who is the actual one who disburses the gifts unto men.

But before ascending to heaven, Christ descended into the lower part of the earth to defeat sin and death. Yet, what exactly does it mean that Christ *went into the lower parts of the earth*?

In the parable of the Rich Man and Lazarus (Luke 16:19-31), Jesus explains that between the torment of

Hades and the comfort of Abraham's bosom (Luke 16:23), a great, impassable gulf is fixed (Luke 16:26).

When Jesus died on the cross, two things happened. First, Christ presented Himself to those Old Testament saints, who were in paradise at Abraham's bosom, allowing them to experience the fulfillment of the promise they died having never seen. Second, Jesus went to the place of torment and tore down the kingdom of the Devil.

Luke writes that one of Christ's purposes in coming to earth, entering time and space as a human baby, was "to preach deliverance to the captives, and...to set at liberty them that are bruised" (Luke 4:18 NIV). In this passage in Luke, Jesus was directly quoting Isaiah 61:1, which reads: "to proclaim liberty to the captives, and the opening of the prison to them that are bound" (NIV).

When Jesus gave up His life on the cross, He (in the Spirit) "went and preached unto the spirits in prison" (1 Peter 3:19 KJV). The word "preached" can be better translated "proclaimed." Jesus proclaimed, or declared His victory over Satan. David had prophetically declared this in Psalm 16:10, writing, "Thou wilt not leave my soul in hell" (KJV). Jesus returned from Hades with "the keys of hell and of death" (Revelations 1:18 KJV) bringing, "captivity captive" with Him as He returned. His spirit returned to His body resting in Joseph's tomb, and He arose from the dead, forever alive.

Jesus defeated every power and principality of Satan, our enemy, rising to life triumphantly at the break of dawn on the third day to the glory of God the Father. He rose with all power and authority (Matthew 28:18), removing the "sting death" (1 Corinthians 15:56 NIV) and ascended to heaven, proclaiming victory over the grave (1 Corinthians 15:57). Jesus Christ has united sinful man with the holy God through His death and resurrection.

John MacArthur explains this magnificent heavenly victory like this:

> *Upon arriving in heaven, He gave gifts to men. Paul here uses yet another term for gifts (domata) to express the comprehensiveness of this gracious provision. Like a triumphant conqueror distributing the spoils to his subjects, so Christ takes the trophies He has won and distributes them in His kingdom. After His ascension came all the gifts empowered by the Holy Spirit (John 7:39; 14:12; Acts 2:33). When the Savior was exalted on high, He sent the Spirit (Acts 1:8), and with the coming of the Spirit also came His gifts to the church.*[4]

What a beautiful picture of the victory of Jesus!

Chapter Summary

God in His omnipotence planned out before the creation of the world how the body of Christ would be unified. He created Adam and Eve and every human after as unique individuals, to be unified in Him. But He also knew it would be impossible for this to happen without His power and grace. This occurred the moment Jesus ascended into Heaven, conquering death and defeating the Devil. Grace was poured out, and the gifts of the Spirit were given to God's people. What were these gifts, and what is their purpose? In the next chapter, we will examine the gifts, and also consider what happens when the Body of Christ is "out of sync."

WORKBOOK

Chapter Three Questions

Question: What kinds of diversity do you see in the body of Christ in your community? Be specific.

Question: What gifts are available to you through Christ?

____
____
____
____
____
____

Question: How do you use your gifts in Christ? To what purposes?

____
____
____
____
____
____
____
____
____
____
____
____

Action: The church is made of people who are different in many ways, whether economically or ethnically, but they are still one in Christ. Receive the gifts that Jesus, who is the head, offers you by grace as a member of His body. God will provide you as His child what you need to do His work in your own unique way—so accept His gifts and use them to serve His purposes, including the unity of the body.

Chapter Three Notes

CHAPTER FOUR

For the Work of the Ministry

And He Himself gave some to be apostles, some prophets, some evangelists, and some pastors and teachers, for the equipping of the saints for the work of ministry, for the edifying of the body of Christ, till we all come to the unity of the faith and of the knowledge of the Son of God, to a perfect man, to the measure of the stature of the fullness of Christ; that we should no longer be children, tossed to and fro and carried about with every wind of doctrine, by the trickery of men, in the cunning craftiness of deceitful plotting, but, speaking the truth in love, may grow up in all things into Him who is the head—Christ—from whom the whole body, joined and knit together by what every joint supplies, according to the effective working by which every part does its share, causes growth of the body for the edifying of itself in love. — ***Ephesians 4:11-16 (NKJV)***

Having been given new life in the resurrection of Jesus, God has graced His people with a great number of different gifts and tasks (Ephesians 4:11-12). He graced some to be apostles, ambassadors, some prophets or evangelists, others pastors and teachers. Regardless of which gifting each member of the Body has been given, it is most important to remember that Paul specifically reminds the Ephesians that each gift is used for:

- The perfecting of the saints
- The work of ministry
- The edifying of the Body

It is at this point that Paul explains how Christ sets about to attain the goal of joining and knitting His Body together with gifted men, purposed to foster and further growth. Paul picks up his thought that he left dangling from Ephesians 4:7, saying "But to each one of us grace was given *according to the measure of Christ's gift....*"

In his book *Body Life*, pastor and theologian Ray Stedman writes that these four gifts listed in Ephesians 4:11-16—apostleship, prophesying, evangelism, and pasturing/teaching—relate to the whole Body of Christ, much as the major body systems relate to the physical body. He writes:

> *Note that each of the four support ministries we are discussing have to do with the Word of God. The first two—apostles and prophets—are concerned with originating and expounding the Word, while the last two--evangelists and pastor-teachers—are concerned with applying the Word to individual lives. The evangelist deals with the beginning of Christian life while the teaching pastor is involved with the development and growth of that life. Evangelists are much like obstetricians, helping to bring new Christians into the world. Teaching pastors are like pediatricians, seeing that these Christians have a healthy spiritual "diet," that their "diseases" receive proper attention, and that they get*

> *plenty of spiritual "fresh air" and "exercise." To return to the word picture of the church as a building, the evangelist is the quarryman who digs out the rock, cuts it loose from quarry stone, and hews it to a rough approximation of its ultimate size. The pastor-teacher is the stone mason who shapes the rock, fitting it into the building in its proper place according to the blueprint of the great architect.*[5]

Paul writes in Ephesians 4:11 that the Lord "gave some." Note that Paul is focusing not on individual *spiritual gifts* but on gifted *persons* who Christ has given to the church. It is the Lord Himself who gives gifted men to the church, to perfect it and move it towards holiness. These men received these gifts for a specific purpose: "to equip his people for works of service, *so that the body of Christ may be built up*" (Ephesians 4:13 NIV, emphasis added).

However, it is not just the "some" that receive gifts. The Lord has gifted each member of the Body of Christ with a specific gifting and function so that "all might come to the unity of faith and knowledge of the Son of God (Ephesians 4:13). Yet, we aren't there yet. Paul writes, "...till we all come to the unity of faith," explaining that this hasn't happened yet.

The members of the Body are still warring with one another, growing more bitter and resentful with each passing moment of strife. We see the evidence in our churches today. But God is at work, bringing them together.

A Body out of Sync

Have you ever noticed when your body is just simply

out of sync? Maybe you can tell by an unusual achiness, or an unfamiliar tightness when you move. Whatever it might be, when we discover that *something* is throwing our body out of sync, we can work to locate the problem and find a solution (whether it be a stomach bug or a broken bone). Then our body can again work as it was made to.

God wants to build up the Body of Christ (Ephesians 4:12). Paul uses an architectural metaphor to make his point: the church is like a building, being "built up" to be the place of God's indwelling. How appropriate, that in Paul's last plea with the church of Ephesus, he reemphasizes this concept of "building up" within the Body. Paul writes, "And now I commend you to God and to the word of His grace, which is able to *build you up* and to give you the inheritance *among all those who are sanctified*" (Acts 20:30 NIV, emphasis added).

When a physical body is sick or out of sync, it cannot be built up. In the same way, the Body of Christ will crumble if its members are disconnected. The temple of the Lord, His dwelling place, needs all of its members working together in order to be built up for His glory, fitted together to form the "building" of God. This is the "unity of the faith" that Paul speaks of in Ephesians 4:12. When one body of doctrinal truth ("the faith") is adhered to, and is lived out in the Body by grace through faith—through believers—there is unity.

As the church at Corinth so clearly illustrates, disunity in the church comes from doctrinal ignorance and spiritual immaturity. Oneness in fellowship is impossible unless it is built

> *on the foundation of commonly believed truth. Paul's solution for the divisions in Corinth was for everyone to hold the same understandings and opinions and to speak the same truths. — **John MacArthur**[6[*

These spiritual ailments may come by means of interacting with people that continually bring you down, or more personally by with the type of media you're listening to, or even the type of shows you watch! When the Body of Christ is not functioning as it was made to, we must work in the unity of the Spirit to locate those ailments and find cures. Sometimes healing comes through forgiveness, through finding a new group of friends, or through keeping a close eye on what sources influence your daily life. God wants to bring healing to the Body so that each of its members is as effective as it can be for the gospel ministry.

The following story by an anonymous author gives an interesting illustration of how one believer not exercising their gift in the Body can affect the message produced by the entire Body.

A Brokxn Kxy

Xvxn though my typxwritxr is an old modxl, it works quitx wxll xxcxpt for onx of thx kxys.

I havx many timxs wishxd that it workxd pxrfxctly.

It is trux that thxrx arx forty-onx kxys that function wxll xnough, but just onx kxy not working makxs thx diffxrxncx.

Somxtimxs it sxxms to mx that our church is

somxthing likx my typxwritxr—not all thx kxy pxoplx arx working propxrly.

As onx of thxm, you may say to yoursxlf, "Wxll, I am only onx pxrson, I don't makx or brxak thx church."

But it doxs makx a big diffxrxncx, bxcasx a church, to bx xffxctivx, nxxds thx activx participation of xvxry pxrson.

So, thx nxxt timx your xfforts arx not nxxdxd vxry much, rxmxmbxr my typxwritxr and say to yoursxlf, "I am a kxy pxrson in thx congrxgation and I am nxxdxd vxry much."

This is what happxns to thx wholx church, and multiply this by many timxs—thx wholx thing just doxs not makx sxnsx!

"Bxlovxd don't bx likx a brokxn kxy."

Growing Up

Each of us, much like little children, must be trained and matured so that we don't eat everything in sight, but only that which is beneficial to our bodies. It's necessary to be trained to try the things we hear and see by the Scriptures in order to know what to listen to and accept in this world we live in. This, as Paul explains to the Ephesians, is what helps us to grow up and to mature in our faith (Ephesians 4:13). Spiritual maturity keeps us grounded and firm, not tossed or carried by crafty sayings or the blowing winds of doctrine.

Infants are not fully mature and thus have underdeveloped body parts. This is okay for a time, until that infant matures. An infant's lung in a grown woman's body would cause severe damage to the rest of her body parts!

Thus, each and every member must be maturely developed in order to benefit the other parts. Spiritually, we're invited to "grow up into him in all things" (Ephesians 4:1 NKJV). Our maturity in God is necessary because every part of the Body of Christ needs the others to function.

It is impossible for the *whole Body* to mature if the *individual parts* are not maturing.

God wants Christians to fulfill the design He intended for each of us when He created the first man and the first woman, Adam and Eve. What fulfillment to be all God originally intended His sons and daughters to be!

God's Intended Plan for His People

What *did* God intend for us to be? Paul tells us clearly in Romans 8:29. God's ultimate plan for His children is that they be "conformed to the image of his Son."

> *For those whom He foreknew he also predestined to become conformed to the image of his Son, that He might be the firstborn among many brothers and sisters.* — ***Romans 8:29 (NIV, emphasis added)***

This is what it means to be a "mature man." This is the end-goal, as a follower of Christ. "Mature" in the original Greek means, "an end, a purpose, an aim, a goal, complete, fully developed, full grown, brought to its end, finished, wanting nothing necessary to completeness, *in good working order*."

When each person in the Body of Christ is in "good working order," the Body can be properly built up.

> *[God] wants a church filled with ordinary men and women who exemplify the extraordinary integrity, temperament, wholeness, compassion, individuality, boldness, righteousness, earnestness, love, forgiveness, selflessness, and faithfulness of Jesus Christ! Deep in your own heart, isn't that what you truly desire? You want to be a whole person, a complete human being. You want to discover and fulfill all that God has built into you...we long to fulfill our humanity, to be the kind of idealized persons that God originally designed us to be. But that is what the church is all about. It is the vehicle designed by God to achieve mature humanity—a humanity exactly like that which was exemplified by the life of Jesus Christ. —* ***Ray Stedman*** [7]

In San Antonio, Texas there rests a historical site known as the Alamo where a great battle for our country was once fought. On a wall near the main entrance to the Alamo is a portrait with the following inscription: "James Butler Bonham—no picture of him exists. This portrait is of his nephew, Major James Bonham, deceased, who greatly resembled his uncle. It is placed here by the family so that people may know the appearance of the man who died for freedom."

Though people will never know what James Butler Bonham looked like *exactly*, they can have an idea, or a "picture" of what he looked like by viewing his nephew.

In the same way, we don't know exactly what God looks like or what His character is like, but we can understand more of who He is by looking at His son, Jesus.

Of course, there is no literal portrait of Jesus either. But we who are filled with the Spirit are called to reflect the image of the invisible God to the world. Paul writes, "And we all, who with unveiled faces contemplate the Lord's glory, are being transformed into his image with ever-increasing glory, which comes from the Lord, who is the Spirit" (2 Corinthians 3:18 NIV).

> *And He put all things under His feet, and gave Him as head over all things to the church, which is His body, the fullness of Him who fills all in all.* ***—Ephesians 1:23 (NKJV)***

Only when its members are functioning well, as the image of Christ, can the Body of Christ be brought "…to the measure of the stature which belongs to the fullness of Christ" (Ephesians 4:13).

> *This may sound selfish, but I trust it is understood. What is the purpose of the church in the world? It is to complete itself that it might grow up.* ***— J. Vernon McGee*** [8]

It is well past the time for the church to grow up.

Chapter Summary

God gave many gifts to the church, including five gifts specific to people who would lead, encourage, and build up the church: apostles, prophets, evangelists, preachers, and teachers. Each of these gifts has a clear purpose, and when one attempts to overtake the other's job, diminish the other's importance, or squash the other, the Body of Christ as a whole does not function. In the same way, God bestows gifts on each individual member of the community. And each member must mature in Christ for the whole body to mature. Only then will God's intended plan for the Body of Christ be fulfilled, which is to be conformed to the image of His son. What does a *mature* believer in Christ look like? What does an *immature* believer look like? What happens when a mature body of believers works together? We'll address this next.

WORKBOOK

Chapter Four Questions

Question: How does forgiveness help you mature in Christ? Where might forgiveness be needed in your life now to help you grow up in Christ?

____
____
____
____
____
____
____
____
____
____
____
____

Question: What are the influences on your daily life? How might you need to make changes in your life with regard to these influences?

____
____

Question: How might others' roles in Christ be dependent on yours? Be specific.

Action: As you embrace the gifts the Lord gives you as a member of His body, seek to grow up in Christ. In order to mature in the Lord, you must learn to seek healing from Him, which comes through forgiveness, a close eye on the sources of influence in your daily life, and a willingness to find new friends if needed. Grow into your role in His body so that your brothers and sisters in Christ can fulfill their own roles and come together in unity of faith and knowledge.

Chapter Four Notes

CHAPTER FIVE

Doctrinal Stability

As a result, we are no longer to be children, tossed here and there by waves and carried about by every wind of doctrine, by the trickery of men, by craftiness in deceitful scheming.
—Ephesians 4:14(NASB)

Paul describes the mature believer in Ephesians 4:14 as one who is not "tossed back and forth by waves, and carried here and there by whatever doctrine fills their itching ears" (2 Timothy 4:3).

In other words, mature believers have their feet firmly on the ground in regard to the teachings of Christ and the fundamental doctrine of the Christian faith. Such an attitude contrasts those "children" who are quickly and easily led astray to deceptive and false heresies. The spiritually immature believer has no roots and is easily blown around by anything new and exciting. Perhaps this is why over and over in Scripture God exhorts us to "stand firm" and "let nothing move you" (1 Corinthians 15:58 NIV), to "stand firm and hold fast to the teachings we passed on to you, whether by word of mouth or by letter" (2 Thessalonians 2:15). Even the prophet Jeremiah spoke of the blessings given to those who root themselves deeply in Christ, the Living Water:

> *Blessed is the man who trusts in the Lord, whose trust is the Lord. He is like a tree planted by water, that sends out its roots by the stream, and does not fear when heat comes, for its leaves remain green, and is not anxious in the year of drought, for it does not cease to bear fruit.* — ***Jeremiah 17:7-8 (ESV)***

Mature believers remain rooted in Christ, and are able to withstand the pressures and untruth that constantly provoke them in this life. Immature believers, however, are "tossed back and forth." That is, they are out of control and are under the influence of external forces, namely, the "waves" of false doctrine and heresy that are often beautifully packaged and intellectually seductive. They are "blown here and there" by the shifting winds of trends and false beliefs.

They are vulnerable to "craftiness," and "deceitful scheming" since they do not have a baseline or foundation of truth by which to adjudicate between competing claims of truth. Paul warns against this in 1 Timothy 1:10.

> *The law is not made for a righteous person, but for those who are lawless and rebellious, for the ungodly and sinners, for the unholy and profane, for those who kill their fathers or mothers, for murderers and immoral men and homosexuals and kidnappers and liars and perjurers, and whatever*

> *else is contrary to sound teaching.* — ***1 Timothy 1:10 (NASB, emphasis added)***

More often than not, what the world says is truth, the word of God says is contrary to sound teaching. Scripture foretold this would happen! Paul, writing to Timothy, said, "The Spirit clearly says that in later times some will abandon the faith and follow deceiving spirits and things taught by demons," (1 Timothy 4:1 NIV).

Rather than being blown around by each new wind, the wise believer will affix himself to the word of God. He "must hold firmly to the trustworthy message as it has been taught, so that he can encourage others by sound doctrine and refute those who oppose it" (Titus 1:9 NIV).

Joined and Knit Together

> *From whom the whole body, joined and knit together by what every joint supplies, according to the effective working by which every part does its share, causes growth of the body for the edifying of itself in love.* — ***Ephesians 4:16 (NKJV)***

God created each of us with a unique function and a unique grace. Though we work differently, we are all "joined and knit together." (Ephesians 4:16 NKJV) This is the beauty of the unified Body of Christ! Our differences are necessary to carry out the task presented to us: the proclamation of the gospel to the world.

Paul reminds his listeners that this "knitting together" must come from Christ. The phrase "from whom" is speaking of the head of the Body: Jesus, from which the entire Body derives its ability to grow. The phrase "being fitted…together" speaks of an intimate union, of being joined together by means of joints—the parts of the Body, or the stones of the building,

> *Every one of them in its own place and function, as the points of connection between member and member, and the points of communication between the different parts and the supply which comes from the Head.* — ***W. Robertson Nicoll***[9]

Jesus is the Master Carpenter, framing a divine building. Different materials may be used—Jews and Gentiles together in Christ, people from different nations and backgrounds—all worshipping the same God and waiting for the return of the same Messiah.

This is an ongoing process! It is why Peter refers to the members of the Body of Christ as "living stones" in 1 Peter 2:5. Through the guiding of the Spirit, we find understanding about the grace given to each of us in order to know exactly how we function. For example, I may not be a foot, but if I'm a knee, I can help the leg to move, the feet to step, the body to walk! If I don't understand my function, I very well may cause the whole body to trip and fall. The body, made up of separate parts, has to be joined as a whole (Psalm 133:1-3).

Part of the Body

Once again, in order for the whole Body to mature, the

individual parts have to be maturing as well. Each part affects the whole. In order for this to happen, Christians must be able to see their responsibility to each other. Paul says in verse 16, "From whom the whole body." Literally, this can be translated "out of whom all of the body."

Perhaps this is why the word of God so often guards against pride, and warns against rebelling against God. It is the nature of humankind to depend only on our self. We think of ourselves as lone islands, capable of doing life without God's help. We miss the revelation that we are only a part of the whole, and that our independence and rebellion pushes against the truth of the Word of God. And then we wonder why the Body of Christ limps along. You and I cannot live like we want to live and escape the fact that *the way we live directly impacts the Body of Christ.*

There is a profound story in the book of Numbers that illustrates this concept. Moses' siblings—Miriam and Aaron—were a bit discontent and grumbling against the Lord. Miriam had started to murmur against Moses to Aaron, and soon the two were together festering in sin.

> *Miriam and Aaron began to talk against Moses because of his Cushite wife, for he had married a Cushite. —* ***Numbers 12:1 (NIV)***

Miriam and Aaron disagreed with Moses, and frankly they needed attitude adjustments. But the Lord was not unaware. He heard their complaining, and was quick to deal with it.

Angry at their squabbling, God commanded the three siblings to meet with Him at the tent of meeting, and disciplined Miriam for her sin—she became terribly leprous, so terrible that Moses described her appearance as a stillborn infant child.

> *So Miriam was shut up outside the camp for seven days, and the people did not move on until Miriam was received again.*
> ***— Numbers 12:15 (NASB)***

One person's sin affected another. Miriam's selfishness and pride brought on God's judgment, which affected not only herself but ultimately a half a million people who were held back for seven whole days until her sin had been dealt with.

Paul likens this to yeast, which causes a whole lump of dough to expand and rise. Yeast, biblically, is a picture of sin:

> *A little yeast works through the whole batch of dough.*
> ***— Galatians 5:9 (NIV)***

What we do affects the whole. Our decisions to obey and to surrender to God affect the whole Body of Christ.

Paul uses the phrase, "by which every part does its share…" (Ephesians 4:16 NKJV). Each member of the Body has a contribution to make. When we understand our purpose and how other parts of the Body mutually benefit each other, we can put an end to the fighting and truly begin to work together. When we understand the unified mission of Jesus Christ, we can stop being intimidated by those who don't look like us or pray like us and start celebrating those differences as beautiful, unique aspects of the family of God.

It is not a matter of contending with one another. It is simply a matter of being what God wants each individual to be. When the body's joints are functioning properly, with every joint contributing to the whole, then the body is being fitted and held together properly. I'm not saying this will be easy! Only when Jesus Christ returns in His fullness will His body also be in its fullness (1 Corinthians 13:10).

Chapter Summary

Mature believers are grounded in the truth of the word of God and are thus able to discern the schemes of the enemy. When you're mature, God knits these "living stones" together into a beautiful dwelling place for Himself, connected to the Head—Jesus Christ—each performing his or her perfectly planned part. On the other hand, when focused on self, the entire body suffers. One person's sin impacts the whole community, like yeast in a lump of dough. Once mature, how should Christians and denominations to operate in relation to one another? Let's consider this in Chapter 6.

WORKBOOK

Chapter Five Questions

Question: What forces are trying to blow you away in your life? What false doctrines do you encounter in the church or in the world?

____
____
____
____
____
____
____
____
____
____
____
____

Question: How can you stay rooted against false doctrines?

____
____
____
____

Question: What does it mean in practice to be knit together with your family in Christ?

Action: As a mature believer, set your feet firmly on the ground in regard to the teachings of Christ. Rather than being blown around by each new wind, affix yourself to the Word of God. Then let yourself be "knit together" with the other members of the body. You cannot live like you want to live or fall prey to the snares of the enemy without negatively affecting the rest of the body of Christ. Understand your purpose in Christ and see your responsibility to your fellow believers so that you can end the infighting and truly begin to work together.

Chapter Five Notes

CHAPTER SIX

Abiding Love

How should each part of the mature Body operate? Paul makes it clear in Ephesians 4:15 that for the Body to mature, believers must be "speaking the truth in love." Literally this phrase can be translated "*truthing* in love," which brings with it the idea of maintaining truth in love, in both in speech and life, or walking in a truthful way. Christians should not just be speaking the truth, but *doing it*. This is the formula by which healthy church growth is maximized.

Paul reminds the Corinthians of this. The formula for healthy growth is faith, hope and, the greatest of these, *love*. (1 Corinthians 13:13) This means that regardless of what we do or who we are, we are called to always operate in love.

"Speaking the truth" pictures the right *doctrine*. "In love" pictures the right *spirit* or *attitude*. We ought to have a great love of the truth and we also ought to do the truth, but we must do the truth in love. Truth without love is harsh treatment, but love without truth is hypocrisy.

Despite our mistakes, God has always met us with an abundance of love and grace. We must learn to walk in the same way. Keep in mind, though, that our enemy wants to fill our minds with unholy guilt for our mistakes. Though it might be tempting, we can't build our faith on guilt and regret. Rather, those mistakes are merely *part* of our story, not the whole. Our faith has been grounded in the redemption of Jesus Christ, in abiding love and grace.

A Whole in the Sky

In 1 Thessalonians 4:17, Paul explains that at the Rapture, believers will meet Jesus Christ in the air. This might seem a trivial point, but consider the chaos that would ensue of Jesus returned to the earth at the door of a church! The headlines would run rampant with Jesus' apparent love for that specific ministry over all the others. This seems so inconsistent with the biblical concept of unity discussed thus far. Consider the beautiful imagery Paul is getting at here: rather than support or ordain one specific ministry, Jesus will draw all men to himself in the clouds, bringing together each part of the unique Body as one whole in the sky!

Knowing Your Part

Every part of the physical body has a law, a specific government. For example, the law of the elbow is different from the government of the feet; the government of the feet is different from the law of the liver, and so on.

We so often view these differences as a means of divisiveness when, in reality, all are needed to function as a whole. The feet can't have the government of eyes, because the eyes don't walk and the feet don't see!

Each of us must know our part and what we're connected to. It's also important to keep in mind that some body parts work best with other specific parts. In other words, there's a fellowship of functions.

Everything you do is in the law of who you are and in the community you are a part of, but this doesn't mean you're restricted to only working with a certain group of people. This diversity is what makes the Christian faith beautiful, because people from different backgrounds and traditions can still fellowship with one another, though they operate differently.

There may be as many denominations and churches as there are parts of the body, because each of them *is* a part! The Body of Christ is so intricately intertwined that understanding your specific part and knowing your unique function is necessary for the whole Body to thrive.

How does the local church fit in to the whole Body of Christ? In ancient Biblical times, there were many local churches, for example, the church at Philippi and Ephesus. How did they fit?

Dr. Wayne Barber believes the following:

> *Since the joint has many bones in it, and in order to function correctly all of them have to be functioning properly, maybe there is a subtle thought here that every local church has to be functioning like a church ought to function. If it doesn't,*

> *then it has rendered the whole body useless as far as its maturing and its growing into the stature of the fullness of Christ.*
>
> *If that is the case, and I don't know if it is or not, what a challenge to us. We need to be a church that is in contact with the Spirit of God, that is listening to the messages from the head which is Christ. We need to daily be filled with the Spirit of God. As we are controlled by the Spirit of God and as we are functioning in our gifts so that every single person is doing what God designed them to do, the whole Body will grow up into what God wants it to be.*[10]

Ephesians 4:16 continues on to say: "according to the proper working of each individual part." Paul is showing the measure by which each individual part participates "according to." In other words, it is going to be according to believers surrendering their spirit to the Spirit of God. When this happens, God is able to pour out His divine supply of gifts to minister to the Body.

As each individual person lets go of their own agenda and allows the Spirit of God to control them, according to the measure they are willing to go, then the whole Body of Christ will grow up and mature into the stature of the fullness of Christ.

It is not a matter of competing with each other; it is about being who God wants each individual to be. When the body's joints are functioning and contributing, then the body is being fitted and held together.

Gifts of mercy, gifts of serving, gifts of compassion—each of these functioning in God's people, through the power of the Spirit of God—enables the Body to embrace the character of Jesus and to reach the stature of the fullness of Christ. Refusing let the Spirit of God control your life halts the process, and immediately affects the whole.

Believers living under the control of the Holy Spirit, "causes the growth of the body for the building up of itself in love" (Ephesians 4:16 KJV).

Perfecting Your Part

So far, we've established that each of us must learn our part in order to serve others. So, how do you serve? Begin by perfecting your part. This comes with knowing what your part requires. If you're an eye, learn how to see. If you're a knee, learn how to bend! Only then will you help the other parts to function as they were created. Then, strive for perfection!

> *All of you together are Christ's body, and each one of you is a part of it. —* ***1 Corinthians 12:27 (NLT)***

This is one reason it is so important to connect to a church family; each of us has a role to play, and each role is divinely significant. Having a good understanding of our specific part and function, we can begin serving those in our immediate community as well as those different parts outside of our community. We need each other to live and work to our fullness.

Ultimately, we do our part and serve others because Jesus served us. Recall how we have discussed our purpose on this earth: to be conformed in the image of Christ (Romans 8:28). Serving others in love is reflecting the image of Christ. Let God fill you with His Spirit, His love, and you won't be able to hold back trying to express it.

How to Serve

Looking at the life of Christ, we can see there are some clear attitudes of the heart necessary to serve like Christ:

In Humility

Chapter 2 of Philippians paints a broad picture of what it means to serve like Christ. We are to consider everyone else better than ourselves, not only with our words, but even in our thoughts. Jesus washed the feet of His disciples, tended to their needs, healed their illnesses, and loved them through their hang-ups. Jesus, the most powerful leader to ever walk this earth, was the greatest servant of all.

> *Do nothing out of selfish ambition or vain conceit. Rather, in humility value others above yourselves, not looking to your own interests but each of you to the interests of the others.*
>
> *In your relationships with one another, have the same mindset as Christ Jesus: Who, being in very nature God, did not consider equality with God something to be used to his own advantage; rather, he made himself nothing by taking the very nature of a servant, being made in human likeness. And being found in appearance as a man, he humbled himself by becoming obedient to death—even death on a cross! —* ***Philippians 2:3-8 (NIV)***

Having the same mind and the same love of Christ unites the Body in spirit.

In Submission

If a person is filled with the Spirit, they are willingly to submit to whatever authority God has placed over them. When we submit ourselves to one another, we are actually bringing honor and glory to Jesus. In Ephesians 5:21, Paul writes, "Submit to one another out of reverence for Christ." It is clear that there is to be a mutual submission between believers, apart from the line of authority. This is the key to healthy, godly relationships. It is the kind of submission Jesus yielded to His Father when He lived on earth as a man. Contrary to human nature, this kind of submission is evidence of the filling of the Spirit.

The actual word for submission, or "be subject to," is *hupostasso* (Gr.) It literally means "to place under in an orderly fashion." It was a military term, illustrating troop divisions arranged in a military fashion under the command of the leader. Those divisions were under clear orders of their commander. Thus, in Ephesians 5, Paul's exhortation for us to submit to one another calls believers to continually and voluntarily place themselves under the authority of each other with Christ as the head.

The only way it is humanly possible for us to carry out this calling is to "be filled with (controlled by) the Spirit" (Ephesians 5:18).

Here is a funny, anonymous story illustrating what Christ-like submission is not:

> *A mild-mannered man was reading a book on being self-assertive and decided to start at home. So he stormed into his house, pointed a finger in his wife's face, and said, "From now on I'm boss around here and my word is law! I want you to prepare me a gourmet meal and draw my bath. Then, when I've eaten and finished my bath, guess who's going to dress me and comb my hair."*
>
> *"The mortician," replied his wife.*

In the Old Testament, King Rehoboam tried this kind of prideful, self-focused leadership, only to find the nation he ruled turning against him. People pleaded for less oppressive taxation, and even Rehoboam's older (and wiser) advisors urged him to consider their requests. However, his young (and likely godless) friends contradicted this wise advice, telling him he should be even more demanding of the people than his father. Rehoboam listened to his friends. The result? Ten of the twelve tribes of Israel seceded and formed a new kingdom (2 Chronicles 10:16-17).

Dare to live life God's way. When you seek to put others ahead of yourself, the pieces begin to fit together the right way, and the Body of Christ functions as it should.

With Unconditional Love

"By love serve one another," Paul taught in Galatians 5:15. Never be conditional in your service. We cannot gain anything out of what we do here on earth, but our Father, who sees our heart, will reward us greatly.

In the book of 1 Corinthians, Paul names a list of services that God Himself has ordained in the church:

> *Now you are the body of Christ, and members individually. And God has appointed these in the church: first apostles, second prophets, third teachers, after that miracles, then gifts of healings, helps, administrations, varieties of tongues. Are all apostles? Are all prophets? Are all teachers? Are all workers of miracles? Do all have gifts of healings? Do all speak with tongues? Do all interpret? But earnestly desire the best gifts. And yet I show you a more excellent way.* ***— 1 Corinthians 12:27-31 (NKJV)***

Then, in Chapter 13, Paul tells us what this "*more excellent way*" is. This more excellent way, *God's way*, is not being full of knowledge, prophetic words, or the ability to perform miracles. Instead, God's way pursues everything in life through the filter of love. Yes, in Christ we have access to those things by the power of *His* Spirit; but without love, each are meaningless. Here is the way of Christ:

> *Love is patient, love is kind. It does not envy, it does not boast, it is not proud. It does not dishonor others, it is not self-seeking, it is not easily angered, it keeps no record of wrongs. Love does not delight in evil but rejoices with the truth. It always protects, always trusts, always hopes, always perseveres. Love never fails.* ***— 1 Corinthians 13:4-8 (NIV)***

Nobody is dispensable. If someone is a hand, then someone else is a leg. Each and everyone has a part to play. Be an encourager of service more than an exploiter of it. Submit to one another out of submission to Christ, in humility, and with His love. And watch the Body of Christ do more than you could ever imagine!

Chapter Summary

Above all, it is paramount that the Body of Christ should operate in the truth of God's Word—in love. As each part of the Body does its part and lets go of his or her agenda, miracles will happen. There simply cannot be competition between individuals or churches. Instead, our attitude towards others should be ones that reflect the image of Christ—such as humility, submission, and unconditional love. When this happens, the Body of Christ will grow. In our final chapter, we will learn how to guard the unique part that God has entrusted to us, and what it means to leave a legacy.

WORKBOOK

Chapter Six Questions

Question: In what areas of your daily life do you struggle to operate in the love of Christ? How could you better reflect Christ in these areas?

____
____
____
____
____
____
____
____
____
____
____
____

Question: How can you better serve others in your life, especially in the body of Christ?

____
____
____
____

____
____
____
____
____
____
____
____

Question: What does it mean to maintain humility toward others? What does it mean to maintain humility toward God?

____
____
____
____
____
____
____
____
____
____
____
____

Action: Don't just speak the truth, but live the truth. This means that regardless of what you do or who you are, you are called to operate in love—always! Keep in mind, though, that our enemy wants to fill our minds with unholy guilt for our mistakes. Though it might be tempting, we can't build our faith on guilt and regret. It is not a matter of competing with each other; it is about being who God wants each individual to be. When the body's joints are functioning and contributing, then the body is being fitted and held together. Serving others in love is reflecting the image of Christ. Let God fill you with His Spirit of love and you won't be able to hold back trying to express it. Encourage service to the Lord and each other, submitting to one another out of submission to Christ. Dare to live life God's way—in love a humility, as His body.

Chapter Six Notes

CHAPTER SEVEN

Guarding Your Part

Striving for spiritual perfection is not easy. Peter reminds us that we have an enemy who desires to contradict us, an enemy always trying to counter our part (1 Peter 5:8). We must always be on guard against the great counter-part. Pinpoint your weaknesses and focus on strengthening those areas, the areas where the enemy is likely to throw you out of sync.

The enemy attacks in many different ways. It's tempting to take on someone else's part in the Body, merely because it looks glamorous or draws a lot of attention. For example, those who teach are quite visible, and often surrounded by others who declare they have been changed by their teaching or moved by their ability to interpret Scripture. Someone with the gift of hospitality may envy the teacher, and may even attempt to teach on occasion. But trying to use a gift that the Lord has not poured in to you is like a person with a degree in art trying to teach calculus to high school students. It's ineffective, and ends up hurting the "whole," more than helping it.

Or maybe you've grown complacent in your part and want to break away from your community, your relationships, or even your job and pursue something that looks more inviting. Yet this is a result of not knowing and being confident in your part. So understand your part, and guard it!

> *Guard the good deposit that was entrusted to you—guard it with the help of the Holy Spirit who lives in us.* ***— 2 Timothy 1:14 (NIV)***

The NASB calls it "the good treasure," given by the Holy Spirit.

Embrace your part—your "good treasure"—and recognize how important it is to God's plan of redemption and to the Body. Guard it with your life.

The way to overcome a counter attack is to ask the difficult questions, to self-examine and to hold our answers to the Scriptures, (2 Corinthians 13:5). We're called to continually ask ourselves whether we are interpreting Scripture accurately. Then, through prayer in the Spirit and examining the word of God, we can guard our part and overcome any attack from the enemy and continue walking in the way of the Lord.

Leaving a Legacy

We all want to leave a lasting legacy. This, too, starts with knowing your specific part and thriving in that part to its fullness. For example, consider John the Baptist.

Having prepared the way for Jesus, he finds himself in prison. Can you feel the disappointment and hopelessness John must have felt? A life's work of preparation culminated in prison walls and doubt! But we know John's legacy to be much more than that.

> *Jesus answered and said to them, 'Go and tell John the things you have seen and heard: that the blind see, the lame walk, the lepers are cleansed, the deaf hear, the dead are raised, the poor have the gospel preached to them.' —* ***Luke 7:22 (NKJV)***

What is Christ saying here? He's saying, "John, you didn't die for nothing! You did your part and because of your work, people are seeing, walking, being cleansed, and being raised from the dead!"

Each of us plays a part in someone else's legacy because we are all connected as a single body. And even though we have limited knowledge of our specific impact, God assures us that we do not work in vain. (1 Corinthians 13:12; 15:58). God connects the parts of the Body for the work of the gospel ministry and assures us of our impact. We will leave a legacy!

Unto Another

Though made up of many members, our bodies exist as one functioning unit. So, it is with the Body of Christ, for by one Spirit we've all been baptized into one body, whether Jew or Gentile, slave or free. All have been made to drink of one Spirit (Galatians 3:28; Colossians

3:11; 1 Corinthians 12:13).

That said, zealously guard against growing arrogant in your part! Keep in mind your constant dependency on others to operate in the fullness of the Spirit, and of their need for you! There is humble reliance within the Body of Christ, a mutual leaning on one another. This is why we must know who we are and who we're connected to, because our work is always unto another, (1 Corinthians 4:7).

Once again, the apostle Paul understood this and spoke about it often in his Epistles. In Romans 9-11, he identifies the Jews and the Gentiles as distinct people groups, each with a very clear part in God's redemptive plan. Israel, according to Isaiah, was created as a nation to be "a light for the Gentiles, that my salvation may reach to the ends of the earth" (Isaiah 49:6 NIV).

The Gentiles, too, have a clear part to play in this grand story. Gentile believers are called to bless the nation of Israel (Genesis 12:3), and to make Israel envious, and as Paul hoped, "somehow arouse [the Jews] to envy and save some of them" (Romans 11:11, 14 NIV).

Notice though what Paul is so adamant about, in regards to the Gentiles. He says to the Gentile believers, "*Do not consider yourself to be superior to those other branches [the nation of Israel]*. If you do, consider this: You do not support the root, but the root supports you" (Romans 11:18 NIV, emphasis added).

Do not become arrogant, Paul says. You each have a part to play, and boasting in superiority over others—especially the nation of Israel—does not build the Body up.

Paul writes, "Can we boast, then, that we have done anything to be accepted by God? No, because our acquittal is not based on obeying the law. It is based on faith" (Romans 3:27).

None of us have reason to boast. Our salvation is based on faith alone, not by who we are, how well we have "kept the law," or by what we have done. How beautiful God's plan is, that it keeps all people in the same position: in a place of necessary humility.

It's futile to think that our specific denomination or community could make up the entire Body of Christ. Salvation is by faith alone, and any person–Jew or Gentile, Baptist or Lutheran, white or black—makes up the Body of Christ *if they believe in Jesus as their Lord and Savior.*

God is always doing more work than we can see or know, in places we'd never think of. If we humbly serve alongside those around us (alike and unlike) and if everyone does their part, the Body will not just live, it will thrive. And if the Body is thriving, the world can be saved!

Lifeblood of the Body

Anatomically, we know that the only part of the body that reaches every member is the blood. We also know that blood cells carry oxygen and nutrients to the whole body, fighting infections and bringing healing to each and every part. The same blood that brings life to the heart brings healing to the stomach; the same blood that brings healing to the stomach reaches the top of your head and the bottom of your foot!

> *For the life of the body is in its blood. —* ***Leviticus 17:11 (NLT)***

Thus, blood is symbolic for life. This is why Jesus' death is such a miracle. Scripture says: "…when Jesus had cried out again in a loud voice, He gave up his spirit" (Matthew 27:50, NIV). Jesus didn't die because He bled to death; He willingly gave up His life for the salvation of the entire world. Jesus gave up His life in exchange for our life. It is Jesus' resurrected life that we share in, and it is this life that connects us as one Body in Him.

In the Church, the uniting force that reaches each and every one of us is the blood (or the life) of Christ. Christ fills, nourishes and heals every member of the body of Christ. Thus, despite our unique differences in background and purpose, the life of Jesus Christ is what brings all parts together as one. Jesus is the lifeblood of the body of Christ, uniting, cleansing and saving those who confide in Him.

A Body in Transition

The church exists as a body in transition, walking the earth with eternity in mind! In fact, Paul reminds us that our citizenship is ultimately in heaven, though we currently live on earth (Philippians 3:20). So, as a collective Body we must begin to prepare for eternity. Whatever your part on earth is—whether a superstar quarterback, a janitor, or a lawyer—an eternity awaits each and every one. Keep in mind, though, that eternity also awaits those who have yet to confess belief in Jesus Christ.

As a church, the Body of Christ has the opportunity to put an end to constant internal bickering and work together to invite the world to turn from sin to holiness. Having established that all people's internal diversity is beautiful and necessary, and that Jesus Christ unites us together through the spirit in our mutual hope, what room is there to continue these petty fights that divide, when the world awaits salvation?

So, as Paul is calling us to in his letter to Ephesus, let us walk as a Body united by the Spirit, graced with diverse purposes and roles, nourished and healed by the blood of Jesus Christ, guarded against our enemy, standing firm in the truth of the Word, being perfected in holiness, and seeking and saving the lost, all the while, working toward leaving a beautiful legacy for Christ.

> *Therefore, my dear brothers and sisters, stand firm. Let nothing move you. Always give yourselves fully to the work of the Lord, because you know that your labor in the Lord is not in vain. — **1 Corinthians 15:58 (NIV)***

WORKBOOK

Chapter Seven Questions

Question: What are your weaknesses that the enemy may be exploiting in your life right now? How could you strengthen these areas?

____

____

____

____

____

____

____

____

____

____

____

____

Question: What is your good treasure in your life? How can you protect it?

____

____

____

Question: What do you think your legacy in Christ is? How might you be able to impact someone else's legacy as part of the body of Christ?

Action: Pinpoint your weaknesses and focus on strengthening the areas where the enemy is likely to throw you out of sync. Embrace your part—your "good treasure"—and recognize how important it is to God's plan of redemption and to the body of Christ. Through prayer in the Spirit and examining the word of God, guard your part—overcoming any attack from the enemy and walking continually in the way of the Lord. Humbly serve alongside those who are like you and those who are not, for if everyone does their part, the body will not just live, it will thrive! Stand firm in the truth of the Word, being perfected in holiness, and seek and save the lost. Work always toward your legacy for Christ.

Chapter Seven Notes

CONCLUSION

The Radical Remnant

The church, the Body of Christ, has fallen asleep, and is desperately in need of restoration. Fortunately, our God is all about reviving and restoring His people. Since the fall of mankind in Genesis, this has been His agenda. He has purposed all things to work out for good and has orchestrated everything to occur as He intended. This includes the church, the Body of Christ. However, how the church currently operates is not how it is ultimately intended to operate.

Unity of the Spirit obligates us to be involved in each other's lives. What God has created through Christ (His church) must be handled delicately. No opinion or preference is worth destroying the Body of Christ.

Like spikes on a wooden wheel, each part of the Body of Christ needs to be working together, one in Spirit and intent, for the whole Body to be functioning in the fullness. If a spoke on a wheel breaks, the whole wheel—in fact the whole cart it supports—is affected. Likewise, one individual or denomination that exists in sin toward another remains broken; thus, the whole body of Christ is affected. How, then, do we pull together as the family of God? In short, we must *do* and *obey*.

> *Do nothing out of selfish ambition or vain conceit. Rather, in humility value others above yourselves, not looking to your own interests but each of you to the interests of the others.*
> ***— Philippians 2:3-4 (NIV)***

Living this way is radical, but it's necessary for spiritual revival and church unity. Division in the Body is one of the key indicators that we are moving quickly toward the return of Christ. Jesus warned us ahead of time that splits and conflict within the church would increase, and would be a sign for those watching and waiting for His soon return.

For this, we should be joyful! Our King is coming soon! Be encouraged that none of this catches God unaware. However, coinciding with this sign within the church will come a time when things not rooted in biblical truth will be unable to withstand a time of shaking. The prophet Haggai warned, "In a little while I will once more shake the heavens and the earth…" (Haggai 2:6 NIV).

This time of shaking is what our Lord identified as the separation of the wheat from the tares (Matthew 13:24-30). Scripture warns of a time when people will love lies and deception more than truth. They will rebel against their Creator, and as a result—in an attempt to motivate them to return to Him—God will discipline so severely, many will not be able to stand.

Will you be part of the remnant that will remain standing? Will you hold fast to the Word of God? Will you trust God and His promises over every temptation that comes your way? Will you live your life according to what He says is His best? Will you commit to being part of the true church of God, one that is without stain, wrinkle or any other blemish?

This is what God has been planning since the beginning of time. He is recreating the assembly of His church. Stand firm, brother and sister. He is coming soon!

> *Just as Christ loved the church and gave himself up for her to make her holy, cleansing her by the washing with water through the word, and to present her to himself as a radiant church, without stain or wrinkle or any other blemish, but holy and blameless.* — ***Ephesians 5:25-27 (NIV)***

Notes

1. Eduard Schweizer. *Exegetical Dictionary of the New Testament*. 3:324.
2. D. Martin Lloyd-Jones. *The Basis of Christian Unity*. Banner of Truth, 2003, p. 27.
3. Wayne Barber. "Ephesians 4:7-10: Preserving the Unity of the Spirit, Part 2." *Preceptaustin.org*. http://www.preceptaustin.org/new_page_19.htm.
4. John MacArthur. *Ephesians*. Moody, 1986.
5. Ray Stedman. *Body Life*. Rev. ed. Discovery House, 1995.
6. John MacArthur. *Ephesians*. Moody, 1986.
7. Ray Stedman. *Ibid.*
8. J. Vernon McGee. *Thru the Bible Commentary*. Thomas Nelson, 1984.
9. W. Robertson Nicoll. *Expositor's Greek Testament*. Ulan, 2012.
10. Wayne Barber. "Ephesians 4:16: Characteristics of Those Who Are Mature in Christ, Part 3." *Preceptaustin.org*. http://ww.preceptaustin.org/new_page_20.htm.

About the Author

Lionel Childress is the fourth child of the late Rev. Tommie and Marlene Childress II. He is a third-generation preacher, born and raised in Houston, Texas.

He had a visitation by God when he was twelve years old, and accepted his call into the gospel ministry at the early age of seventeen after his oldest brother was shot and killed. This changed his life, and following his brother's death he vowed to God to save lives.

Shortly after, he joined in matrimony to his beautiful wife, Jeanette Denson Childress, now of forty years. They then moved to Marshall, Texas, to pursue college. While in college, he pastored two CME Methodist churches as well as teaching a class in college, of which many still talk about to this day. He also preached and evangelized in every city and state, and every church and denomination he could.

He and his wife have seven lovely birth children, of which one, Shantocqua NaKim, is now in heaven along with their adopted son Schon J. Vaughn. They have several adopted sons and daughters, with children of their own, and Lionel has many God-children also. He has a great heart for God and God's people.

He is a Doctor of Divinity, Apostle, and Bishop, as well as a pastor, evangelist, prophet, teacher, and counselor. After college, he founded and established Childress Deliverance Temple Ministries in July 1989, named in honor of his father. He is also the Father and Covering of Childress Covenant International, which now covers over thirty-eight churches across the world.

His true belief is nondenominational, meaning that we all make up part of the Body of Christ. No one ministry knows all or has all of who God is. He's been around a long time preaching this gospel. He's not tired yet.

His all-time favorite words of encouragement include "Love has no color," "All is well," "The devil is defeated," "Moving forward under an open heaven," and many more. He is known everywhere for his powerful preaching, teaching, old-time singing in his deep bass voice, shouting, dancing, praying, fasting, prophecy, miracles, wisdom, revelations, and most of all, his love.

He has had several visions of heaven and hell, and of our Lord and God. When he preaches, he says, "*Do you believe it? Say Amen.*" Then, in the pulpit and at home, and everywhere and anywhere, when he talks to anyone he says, *"Glory"*—all the time.

He truly lives a save and sanctified life for God and is full of the Holy Ghost. Humble in every way, he is continuing to move in the vision God gave him. Though his vision is not perfect, with and by God's Grace upon his life, the vision continues to unfold. Now, as he would say, *"Do you believe it? Say Amen. Glory!"*

About SermonToBook.Com

SermonToBook.com began with a simple belief: that sermons should be touching lives, not collecting dust. That′ s why we turn sermons into high-quality books that are accessible to people all over the globe.

Turning your sermon or sermon series into a book exposes more people to God′ s Word, better equips you for counseling, accelerates future sermon prep, adds credibility to your ministry, and even helps make ends meet during tight times.

John 21:25 tells us that the world itself couldn′ t contain the books that would be written about the work of Jesus Christ. Our mission is to try anyway. Because in heaven, there will no longer be a need for sermons or books. Our time is now.

If God so leads you, we′ d love to work with you on your sermon or sermon series.

www.ingramcontent.com/pod-product-compliance
Lightning Source LLC
Chambersburg PA
CBHW061832040426
42447CB00012B/2941

* 9 7 8 1 9 4 5 7 9 3 3 2 5 *